A Lamp Unto My Feet

Ginny Breecher

ISBN 978-1-63903-868-8 (paperback)
ISBN 979-8-88540-130-2 (hardcover)
ISBN 978-1-63903-869-5 (digital)

Copyright © 2022 by Ginny Breecher

All rights reserved. No part of this publication may be reproduced, distributed, or transmitted in any form or by any means, including photocopying, recording, or other electronic or mechanical methods without the prior written permission of the publisher. For permission requests, solicit the publisher via the address below.

Christian Faith Publishing
832 Park Avenue
Meadville, PA 16335
www.christianfaithpublishing.com

Watercolor by Ginny Breecher

Printed in the United States of America

Your word is a lamp unto my feet, a light upon my path.

—Psalm 119:105 (NIV)

With profound gratitude, I recognize the following people who have inspired, encouraged, and supported me as I learned how to put what was stirring in my heart into lyrics and music. Jean Sweeney, my musical neighbor, as well as Peggy Crawford, beloved Hough Street School music teacher, patiently answered my endless questions. At Messiah Lutheran Church in Wauconda, Illinois, Pam Dadian, our church's talented director of music, instructed, encouraged, and supported me with what can only be described as amazing grace. Many thanks to all Messiah's pastors throughout the years, especially Pastor Chuck Merkner, Pastor Lynne Morrow, and Pastor Steve Swanson for their constant inspiration. To God be the glory! And all God's people said, "Amen!"

Contents

Your Word	7
Listen to the Stillness	8
He	9
Come	10
God of Love	11
From the Ashes	12
A Humble Heart	13
Look for the Joy!	14
A House of Prayer	15
King of Glory	16
With My God!	17
Sharing Jesus' Love	18
The Blessing	19
Make Me a Blessing!	20
Joy in the Morning	21
The Answer	22
Bless this House	23
Do Not Fear!	24
Changing	25
And Darkness Fell	26
In God We Trust	27
Shine for Jesus!	28
Bloom Where You Are Planted!	30

Your Word

Your Word's a lamp unto my feet
That guides me through each day.
It's the light in every shadow that I face;
A beacon in the darkness so all will see,
A glimpse of Your amazing grace,
A glimpse of Your amazing grace.

It's my refuge through the storms of life
That challenge me today.
It's the rock where I will always take my stand;
The hope that lives within me that promises,
My life's forever in Your hands.
My life's forever in Your hands.

Ginny Breecher ©2021

Listen to the Stillness

Listen, listen to the stillness;
For the voice of God you'll hear.
If you listen in the stillness,
You will know His love is near.
Listen, listen when He tells you,
You are precious in His eyes.
He will comfort and protect you.
He will answer when you cry.
Listen, listen to God speaking;
For His words are meant for you.
Let the peace of God flow through you,
As your spirit is renewed.
Listen, listen to the stillness.
Listen with your heart and soul.
Listen in that gentle silence for
His love will make you whole.

Ginny Breecher ©1997

HE

A Savior born of humble birth,
Filled the hearts and souls of men on earth,
Bringing peace and hope and goodwill to all,
Love and joy to those who hear Him call.

He walked the hills of Galilee,
And He spoke the words that calmed the sea,
And He prayed for me at Gethsemane,
Then He gave His life to set me free.

He taught us how to know His will,
How to trust His Word to guide us still,
How to reach for those who've
Lost their hope,
Lost their way,
How to love them when we pray.

His mighty voice, creation stirred,
And my heart, His whisper understood.
In the stillness, He is calling me, loving me,
Now and for eternity.

Ginny Breecher ©2007

Come

Come and see, come and see,
That the Lord is good.
He grants us peace, brings us hope,
According to His Word.
His Light shines in the darkness just for you and me.
Come and see. Come and see.

Come to Me, come to Me,
With your brokenness,
And I will comfort your heart,
Your weary soul give rest.
For I have loved you, My child, throughout eternity.
Come to Me. Come to Me.

Come and be, come and be,
All you're meant to be.
The plans I've made for your life
Will set your spirit free.
My Light will shine in your heart for all the world to see.
Come and be. Come and be.

Ginny Breecher ©2021

God of Love

God of Love, God of Grace,
Hear now the prayer that we offer.
Your humble servants, praising Your Name,
Your wondrous love to proclaim.

God of Hope, God of Peace,
Fill us with Your Holy Spirit.
Guide Thou our lives, so all that we do,
Always brings Glory to You.

God of our Fathers, Ancient of Days,
Your Word, we trust still to obey.
Search now our hearts, that blameless we be,
Worthy to walk Lord with Thee.

Ginny Breecher ©2013

From the Ashes

From the ashes of my life, make something strong.
I have tried to hide in darkness far too long.
Turn my heart toward You,
My feet away from what I know is wrong.
From the ashes of my life, make something strong.

From the ashes of my life, make something good,
As I struggle through my days, misunderstood.
Help me learn to trust Your mercy
And the power of Your Word.
From the ashes of my life, make something good.

From the ashes of my life, make something new.
When this world looks at me, let them see You.
Let me shine for You, O Jesus,
With a life that honors You.
From the ashes of my life, make something new.

Through the ashes of my life, I've felt Your love,
In the victory that's mine through Christ above.
For there's nothing that can separate me from my Savior's love.
Through the ashes of my life, I know I'm loved.

Ginny Breecher ©2005

A Humble Heart

Blessed Jesus, my heart belongs to You.
May it faithful and humble be.
May my words, my deeds, bring honor to You.
May my life, a tribute be.

May I understand more fully, Lord,
What it means to follow Thee.
More of You, dear Father, less of me;
Learning true humility.

Help me realize each day I live,
Is a wondrous gift of love.
With a grateful heart and soul I give,
Myself to You in love.

May this Holy season bring to me,
Opportunity anew.
May each life I touch see reflected in me,
A heart that shines for You.

Ginny Breecher ©1998

Look for the Joy!

Look for the joy in each passing day.
Look for the smile of God.
Watch for a glimpse of His wondrous love,
Shining in your child's eyes.

Look for the love in your daily life.
Watch for the hand of God.
Watch as the love that you give away,
Flows back in blessings to you.

Look for the joy in the face of a friend.
Watch for the spirit of God.
Watch as the love of God overflows,
Touching and healing mankind!

He sends His love in such special ways.
Look for the joy every day!

Ginny Breecher ©1997

A House of Prayer

Make this house a house of prayer,
So that all who gather here;
Will reflect a Light that's brighter than the sun,
As they feel Your Presence near.

Make my heart a heart of prayer,
Open always, Lord, to hear.
Keep me faithful to Your never changing Word
And the Truth that I find there.

Make my life a life of prayer,
Daily trusting in Your care.
Grant me strength and wisdom, Lord, to do Your will,
As Your wondrous love I share.

Make this house a house of prayer,
Filled with power beyond compare.
For we know that there is nothing we can't do,
When we put our trust in You.

Ginny Breecher ©2009

King of Glory

Even though the path is long,
Filled with choices, right or wrong,
I will put my trust in God above
And in His unfailing love.

It's the power of the cross,
That reminds us we are not lost.
Every step we take in the Father's will,
Draws us closer, closer still.

Precious Jesus, I am free,
Free to follow You willingly.
You reached out in mercy and rescued me,
Now my heart, I give to Thee.

King of Glory, reign in me.
May my life be Your victory.
Let Your light so shine in this heart of mine,
Shine for You, O Jesus, Shine!

Ginny Breecher ©2009

With My God!

With my God, all things are possible,
For by His Word, He tells me I'm His own.
And with my God, there is nothing I can't do,
For all things are possible!
Yes, all things are possible!

With my God, I never walk alone;
His Word, the lamp that lights my path toward Home.
And with my God, there is nothing I can't do,
For all things are possible!
Yes, all things are possible!

He is here each time I kneel to pray,
And He is here to guide me every day.
And with my God, there is nothing I can't do,
For all things are possible!
Yes, all things are possible!

With my God, all things are possible.
I live beneath the shadow of His wings.
And with my God, there's no mountain I can't climb,
For all things are possible!
Yes, all things are possible!

Jesus Christ brings hope to you and me.
His sacrifice still sets believers free!
And in His Name, there is nothing we can't do,
For all things are possible!
In Jesus' Name, all things are possible!

Ginny Breecher ©2014

Sharing Jesus' Love

Be the hope for the hopeless,
The strength for the weak.
Be a shoulder to cry on,
A voice for those who cannot speak.
Be a light in the darkness, a candle of truth,
As together we share Jesus' love.
With our arms wide open to comfort you,
Reaching out as Jesus would do.

Be a home for the homeless, a shelter from pain.
Be the food for the hungry.
Feed the soul of every man.
Be a friend to the lonely, a listening ear,
Touching hearts that to Jesus are dear.
Let the Father's compassion awaken in you,
And reach out as Jesus would do.

Be a refuge for wandering souls, lost and alone.
Be the hand they reach out for,
Gently guiding them toward Home;
Sharing hope for tomorrow, love long overdue,
As they come to know Jesus through you.
May the love of the Father be reflected in you,
Reaching out as Jesus would do.

Ginny Breecher ©1998

The Blessing

Let your light so shine in the darkness;
With His love, your heart overflow.
May the peace that exceeds understanding
Fill your life, your heart, and your soul.

May the Spirit of God guide your footsteps.
May you walk in His will day by day.
May the prayer in your heart become yearning
To live for Jesus always.

May you trust each promise He gives you.
May you choose every day to obey.
May His strength and His wisdom stay with you,
And the joy of His love light your way.

Ginny Breecher ©2002

Make Me a Blessing!

Make me a blessing, Lord,
An instrument of peace.
Where hatred lives in angry hearts,
Your healing love release.

Make me a blessing, Lord,
An instrument of truth,
A still, small voice, the gentle roar,
That's heard throughout the earth.

Make me a blessing, Lord,
An instrument of grace,
In lovingkindness reaching out,
So all will see Your face.

Your servant, I will be.
Send me, O Lord, send me,
To spread the good news of Your Love,
Across eternity.

For Jesus is our Hope,
Our Life, our Truth, our Way;
Our Refuge in the wilderness,
The Joy of each new day.

Ginny Breecher ©2010

Joy in the Morning

Joy in the morning, so precious and new,
Loving You, Jesus, belonging to You.
Living each day as a child of the King,
Joyfully, now I sing.

Heavenly Father, Spirit above,
Fill now my heart with Your wondrous love.
Mercy, forgiveness, flow gently o'er me,
Love, unconditionally.

Teach me to trust You, to trust and obey.
Guard every footstep, each word that I say.
Lead me to those who are longing for grace,
Longing for Your embrace.

Use me, O Father, to follow Your will.
Speak, and my heart will be perfectly still.
Prayers of thanksgiving before You I bring,
My life, my offering.

Ginny Breecher ©2006

The Answer

Refresh my soul with Living Water.
Restore me with the Bread of Life.
You are the Way, the Truth, the Answer,
The Living Word that guides my life.

You are my Rest when I grow weary.
When I'm afraid, you calm my fears.
When I cry out, in need of comfort,
You are the Hand that wipes my tears.

You are my Rock and my Salvation.
You are my Strength, for I am weak.
Your Voice can still my troubled waters.
My heart rejoices when You speak.

You are Creator and Redeemer.
You are the Wind beneath my wings.
You are the Light upon my pathway;
The joyful Song that my soul sings!

You are the Vine that my heart clings to;
The Peace reflected on my face.
You are the Breath of life within me,
O God of Mercy, God of Grace.

You are the Hope of every nation;
The Hope that lives in every heart.
You are the Answer through the ages,
O God of Love, bright Morning Star.

Ginny Breecher ©2020

Bless this House

Bless this house, bless this people,
As we worship here today.
Let the Light of Your Spirit shine in all we do and say.
Bless each child, man, and woman as our joyful praises ring.
With our hearts overflowing, Father, hear us sing!

Grant us peace, sanctuary,
As we struggle through each day.
Give us strength for the journey.
Hear us, Father, when we pray.
Guide us, Lord, through the darkness of
a world where hope seems lost.
And in all things, remind us, to lift high the cross.

Bless this house, bless this people,
To the Glory of Your Name.
Fill our lives with one purpose,
To the world Your Love proclaim.
Touch each heart with Your mercy, fill
each empty soul with grace,
'Til the love of the Savior shines on every face!

Ginny Breecher ©2004

Do Not Fear!

Do not fear the darkened path before you,
For we're children of the Light,
And your Heavenly Father's arms will shelter you
Through the dark and endless night.

He'll be there when morning breaks above you,
And He'll guide you through each day.
When your heart grows weary, He will carry you,
Every step along the way.

Wrapped in peace that passes understanding,
I will follow where You lead.
Precious Jesus, You have taught my soul to sing.
You are all the Hope I need.

Ginny Breecher ©2016

Changing

God is changing hearts, one at a time.
He is changing yours; He is changing mine.
The love of Jesus has set us free,
To be all He calls us to be.

God is changing lives, day after day.
If we follow Him, we will not lose our way.
He has promised that He will never leave.
Trusting Him, this we believe.

God is searching hearts, one at a time.
May He find mine humble and gentle and kind.
Shining with the love He has given me,
Love that all the world can see.

God is calling you, day after day,
To be salt and light; to be people who pray.
To reach out as He once reached out for you;
To love, as He first loved you.

Ginny Breecher ©2007

And Darkness Fell

And darkness fell on the Garden of Gethsemane,
On a Heart torn by anguish and love.
And darkness fell on the Lamb of Calvary,
While angels gathered in silence above.
And darkness fell on a face etched in agony,
Nailed to a cross, sacrificed willingly.
And darkness fell as the Body gave up its fight,
But darkness couldn't extinguish The Light!

Ginny Breecher ©1998

In God We Trust

Psalm 91 (NIV)

In God we trust, in Him alone.
He knows our hearts; we are His own.
Though arrows threaten us by day,
And terrors possess the night;
He lifts us up on eagle's wings
And keeps us in His sight.

In God we trust, whose mighty hand
Delivers us from evil's plan.
Our refuge and our fortress be,
In a world paralyzed by fear.
Though thousands fall before our eyes,
We know our God is near.

When all around us lose their way,
We kneel to worship and to pray.
For we are children of the Lord,
Beloved in His sight.
We stand together, hand in hand,
In the warmth of Holy Light.

Ginny Breecher ©9/11/2001

Shine for Jesus!

Be the Light the world can see,
Shine for Jesus!
Spread the wonder of His Love across the land.
Reach the hopeless and the lost
With the power of the cross.
Be the Light, the Love of Christ, for all to see!

Be the Light the world can see,
Shine for Jesus!
Be the hand that reaches out in Jesus' Name.
Where there's worry, calm the fears.
Where there's sorrow, wipe the tears.
Be the Light, the Love of Christ, for all to see!

Be the Light the world can see,
Shine for Jesus!
Share the hope within your heart, reach out, reach out.
Serve with grace and dignity,
Homeless, hungry, refugee.
Be the Light, the Love of Christ, for all to see!

Be the Light the world can see,
Shine for Jesus!
Be the gentle voice that shares the Savior's Love.
Where life's brokenness is found,
Jesus' healing love abounds.
Be the Light, the Love of Christ, for all to see!

You're the Hope that fills our hearts, Precious Jesus.
You're the Peace that overflows throughout our lives.
We are children of the Light,
Safe, secure within Your sight.
You're the Life. You are the Truth. You are our Way!

Ginny Breecher ©2020

Bloom Where You Are Planted!

Written for Messiah's HUGS Ministry

Clothe yourself in kindness, grace, humility.
Share the love of Jesus so this broken world will see.
Be the light in the darkness, shining with His Love.
Bloom where you are planted, sharing the Savior's Love!

Reach the lost and lonely. Comfort those who mourn.
Listen with compassion to the weary and forlorn.
Be the light in the darkness, shining with God's love.
Bloom where you are planted, sharing the Savior's Love!

Each new day is alive with possibilities.
Guide my words, my footsteps so my heart's where it should be.
Let my life be a beacon, shining with Your love,
Blooming where I'm planted, sharing my Savior's Love!

Through this present darkness, Jesus, You are near.
We can feel Your Presence, in each smile, each hug, each tear.
We will light up the darkness with Your unfailing love;
Blooming where we're planted, proof of our Savior's Love!

Ginny Breecher ©2020

About the Author

Ginny Breecher has been writing praise and worship hymns for area churches for twenty-seven years. She has enjoyed playing with the bell choir at Messiah Lutheran Church in Wauconda, Illinois. She is a past Stephen Minister and hospice volunteer.

When not at her piano, you can find her working in her garden or painting in the art room. She loves spending time with her grandchildren, working on art projects or creating beautiful music together. Now retired, she lives with her husband, Tom, in Barrington, Illinois.

A Lamp Unto My Feet represents a small collection of the poetry from some of her hymns.

CPSIA information can be obtained
at www.ICGtesting.com
Printed in the USA
JSRC022123030322
R11481300001B/R114813PG23442JSX00001B/1